with this ring

with this ring

the ultimate guide to wedding jewelry

PENNY PRODDOW

MARION FASEL

Illustrations by Sukhee Ko

Special Photography by Darrin Haddad

Bulfinch Press   New York • Boston

Bulfinch Press
Time Warner Book Group
1271 Avenue of the Americas
New York, NY 10020
Visit our Web site at www.bulfinchpress.com

First Edition

Library of Congress Cataloging-in-Publication Data
Proddow, Penny.
With this ring: the ultimate guide to wedding jewelry / Penny Proddow and Marion Fasel ; illustrations by Sukhee Ko. — 1st ed.
    p.   cm.
Includes index.
ISBN 0-8212-2886-2
1. Diamonds — Purchasing. 2. Rings — Purchasing. 3. Weddings — United States — Planning. 4. Jewelry — United States — History.
I. Fasel, Marion. II. Title.
HD9677.A2P76 2004
392.5'4 — dc22   2003027837

Designed by Nina Barnett

Printed in China

contents

here comes
the sparkle

Always keep a diamond in your mind.

— Tom Waits

Jewelry begins and ends it all. A ring officially announces you are engaged. Another ring says you are married. Between these bookend pieces there can be more razzle-dazzle with precious wedding presents and wedding day jewelry. In other words, getting married means at least two new jewels in your life and maybe more. One mission of this book is to make sure you are not blinded by the light but bask in it.

There are three chapters, each divided broadly into the same three parts: the rings, precious wedding presents, and wedding day jewelry. They all illuminate different facets. The first chapter, Storybook Style, is a historical glance back at what it was like once upon a time. The second, Celebrity Style, is a scrapbook of larger-than-life women and their extravagant and intimate pieces. These chapters unveil traditions and trends and the fabulous legacy of wedding jewelry. The third chapter, Your Style, is a close-up look at designs and the hard facts you should know before buying jewelry to celebrate your engagement and wedding.

Jewelry has long been an important part of getting married. Why? Jewelry has a magical ability to carry memories. It is beautiful, personal, meaningful, valuable, symbolic, and it endures. When the fairy dust settles after the pageantry, the jewelry still shines brightly. Jewelry is a part of what you have and hold. Quite simply, jewelry is joy. This book, above all else, is designed to help you make the jewelry decisions of a lifetime and have the time of your life doing it.

storybook
STYLE

history and traditions

Romantic and fanciful, the history of wedding jewelry seems like a tale straight out of a child's storybook. Enchanting imagery and hidden messages were scrolled all over old engagement rings. They were on the inside and outside of bands and even in secret compartments. Great jewelry treasures shone among a bride's wedding presents. And there was sparkle supreme on the wedding day, when a bride appeared before the groom and all her guests in amazing finery. Every bit of precious jewelry, from the ring to the tiara, was full of symbolism, a story really about the greatest hopes and dreams for a marriage.

THE RINGS

Once upon a time, no one is sure exactly when, a ring became a token of marriage. Who thought of it first or where the custom originated may never fully be known. The tradition was under way in ancient Rome, where many brides wore a simple band of iron. People believed the circle of the ring symbolized eternal love. Over the centuries, the wedding ring custom was adopted throughout the western world. The symbolism changed to different messages of faith and love, and the design evolved into exquisite rings made of gold and gems. Sometimes the ring was given before the wedding ceremony and other times during it. The concept of two rings—an engagement ring and a wedding band—came into vogue in the eighteenth century in England and has never gone out of style.

Through it all, change was the constant. Designs were altered countless times. The finger a bride wore her ring on switched repeatedly. What continued on and on was the ring itself. It became the ultimate symbol that a woman had wed or planned to do so soon.

A key engagement ring opened the marriage chapter to many women's lives in ancient times. During the third century in Rome, a key engagement ring was made of brass, bronze, or iron. It celebrated a bride's entrance into her husband's home and sharing in his possessions. Special key rings actually opened little locks on jewelry boxes. The style kept its appeal for couples over centuries in different parts of Europe. In England during the sixth century, a Saxon bride received a key engagement ring and other valuables, including keys to her new house which she wore around her waist. The keys, a symbol of trust and responsibility, were mentioned in the wedding service by the father of the bride: "I give thee my daughter to be thy honor and thy wife, to keep thy keys, and to share with thee in thy bed and goods."

In the fifteenth century, precious gems debuted in gold engagement rings. Royalty, men and women alike, flaunted their gems flamboyantly. Each stone had a meaning that was known among society. The ruby read as exalted love. An emerald was full of hope. Diamonds, the top choice, sparkled with the purity of fidelity and durability. During this time the shape of diamonds in rings was a pyramid. Gem cutters had just enough skill to take a diamond octahedron (the natural form of the gem, which looks like two pyramids joined at the base), cleave it in half, and polish the sides.

There were hidden messages and a trick opening on gimmel engagement rings. A stylish choice among well-to-do brides from the fifteenth through the seventeenth centuries, the gold ring had two rectangular gems on top, usually a diamond and a ruby for commitment and passion. Upon occasion satyrs and nymphs were depicted in colorful enamel just below the stones, as metaphors for a playful courtship. When a couple became engaged, the ring was split evenly into two parts, using the trick opening on the band. The woman wore half and her fiancé wore the other half. During the engagement period the messages on the interior of the band were exposed. One favorite phrase came from the wedding ceremony, engraved in Latin: "What God has joined together let no man put asunder." It matched the design of the ring and fit the moment during the ceremony when the groom took his half of the ring and joined it with his bride's half before slipping the whole ring onto her finger.

Sixteenth-century j e w i s h   w e d d i n g   r i n g s made in Italy and Germany were wonderfully elaborate. Set on top of a wide gold band was a miniature temple of gold and colorful enamel with a Moorish dome or slanted roof. Many of the little roofs opened to show the words *mazel tov,* good luck in Hebrew. There were messages around the band for good fortune or depictions of sacred stories. The large and heavy rings were ceremonial. They were not worn every day but kept in family collections or the temple treasuries.

The romantic Irish c l a d d a g h   r i n g has two hands holding a heart with a crown. During the eighteenth century the design was used as an engagement ring in the fishing village of Claddagh on the western coast of Galway, but the motif didn't originate there. It was a fancy court style set with diamonds in seventeenth-century Italy. The Irish adopted it, re-created it in gold, and named it after the fishing village. Frequently the rings were engraved with the alternating letters of the couple's first names, one reading from the right and the other from the left. For example, George and Sophia would be GaEiOhRpGoEs. Claddagh engagement rings were passed down through generations from mother to daughter.

diamond engagement rings

reigned in the extravagant courts of eighteenth-

century Europe. Their ascendancy came

from many things: sheer beauty, status,

the tradition of sentiments attached to the

stone (fidelity and durability), and

the steady supply of gems from the newly

discovered diamond mines in Brazil. While

noblewomen had large diamond earrings, tiaras, necklaces, and bracelets,

their diamond engagement rings were delicate. They frequently had a small

center stone and two side stones set in silver on a slender gold band.

It was during this time that a second ring joined the engagement ring. The
newcomer was not officially a wedding band. Queen Charlotte,

wife of George III of England and nicknamed the Queen

of Diamonds, simply decided to combine a

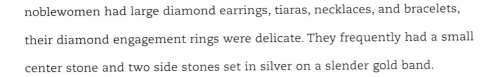

diamond band with her engagement ring.

The bright idea of two rings caught on and

eventually became a tradition, with an

engagement ring given at the moment of the

proposal and a wedding band during the ceremony.

The simply stunning t i f f a n y   s e t t i n g, invented in 1886, changed the style of engagement rings forever. Prongs lifted a round diamond up from a plain gold band, letting light pass through the gem and heightening its brilliance. Charles Lewis Tiffany, the mastermind behind the setting, knew that to Americans diamonds were symbols of royalty, pomp, and circumstance much more than tokens of fidelity and durability. The Tiffany Setting emphasized the glory of a diamond. It was a clear statement, without any superfluous details, of what a couple wanted to represent their marriage.

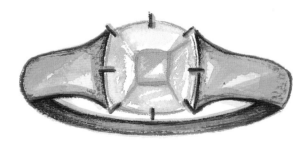

THE RINGS: Facts on the Fingers

E ngagement rings and wedding bands have been worn on many different fingers of the right and left hands. The reasons for these differences were usually romantic or religious but have sometimes been purely practical.

left hand

The **third finger of the left hand** has long been the most well known and popular location for engagement rings and wedding bands. In Roman times people put an engagement ring on this finger because they believed there was a vein, called the vena amoris, connecting it to the heart. During fifteenth- and sixteenth-century Christian wedding ceremonies, the priest touched the ring to the **thumb and each of the first two fingers** of the bride's left hand while he recited the Trinitarian formula: In the name of the Father, the Son, and the Holy Ghost. He slipped the ring on the **third finger of her left hand** as he said

Amen. Historians have attributed the popularity of the left ring finger to the fact that it is the least active finger for most people — except lefties of course — and therefore the best place to showcase a beautiful jewel.

In England during the seventeenth century the wedding ring was put on the **third finger of the left hand** during the ceremony. Afterward the bride wore it on any finger she chose. The **thumb of the left hand** was a popular choice. Every joint on the fingers was dedicated to a particular saint, and the second joint of the thumb was for the Virgin Mary.

right hand

Large sixteenth-century Jewish wedding rings were placed on the **index finger of the right hand** during the ceremony. They were ceremonial and not worn after the event.

From the eleventh to the fifteenth century in France, the wedding ring was worn on the **second or third finger of the right hand** because people believed that one or both of these fingers had veins connected to the heart.

In Greece there has been a continuous tradition of wearing the engagement ring on the **third finger of the left hand** before the wedding. During the ceremony the priest moves the ring **to the third finger of the right hand,** where it remains. Greeks believe the right hand is blessed because it is the hand the priest uses when he makes the sign of the cross.

PRECIOUS WEDDING PRESENTS

It has always been considered a grand gesture and quite fitting to give a bride a precious wedding present — a special piece that shines and endures. The tradition has been around at least as long as the ritual of the ring. Mythic motifs, legendary lovers, the simple language of flowers, and a dove are just a few of the designs that have played a part in great bridal gifts through the ages.

Brides in ancient Greece had beautiful jewelry. It is well documented in the pictures on black figure and red figure vases, which chronicled daily life. One type of jewel Greek brides received as a wedding gift was a gold knot of hercules necklace set with semiprecious stones such as amethysts or garnets. The famous ancient knot has two interlocking loops joined in a virtually unbreakable bond.

p e a r l s were the ultimate wedding present among sixteenth-century European nobility. The marine gems were associated with Aphrodite, the goddess of love, and symbolized innocence, purity, and perfection. At the time, pearls were also extremely rare. There was no such thing as cultured pearls or systematic pearl farming. Each and every pearl had to be found by divers and then imported to Europe by boat or caravan from as far away as Panama or the Indian Ocean. Because of their immense value, each pearl gift was well documented among a bride's presents. Catherine de Médicis received six ropes of pearls from her uncle Pope Clement VII and 92- and 96-grain pearls from her father-in-law-to-be, King Francis I of France. The 203.84-grain Peregrina pearl, one of the most famous pearls in the world, was a wedding present from King Philip II of Spain to his bride, Mary I of England. The English queen wore the large pear-shaped pearl suspended from a chain on her wedding day.

The love match and 1840 marriage of Queen Victoria to Prince Albert in England began an era of sentimental jewelry. Clasped-hand brooches, heart-shaped pendants, and cameos with cupids were among the sweet themes.

enamel-and-gold flower brooches,

a fashionable gift for brides from grooms, were like little love letters with specific sentiments. The rose equaled love. Mistletoe was the equivalent of a kiss. And daisies added innocence to the bouquet.

The Pre-Raphaelite painter Edward Burne-Jones collaborated with master jewelers Carlo and Arthur Giuliano on a symbolic brooch for the bridesmaids at his wedding. The brooches featured Venus's attendant, a d o v e , with a coral cabochon body and turquoise cabochon wings and tail, perched on a green enamel olive tree, a symbol of peace and tranquillity.

WEDDING DAY JEWELRY

For hundreds and even thousands of years — probably since the dawn of civilization — brides have worn jewelry on their wedding day. There is no doubt about it. Countless brides have been beautifully accessorized through the ages and around the world. But in three epic times and special places — ancient Greece, sixteenth-century India, and nineteenth-century England — brides wore jewelry so dazzling, intricate, and imaginative that their looks have become legendary.

The bride in ancient greece was all romance and poetry on her wedding day. Her dress was purple, a favorite of the lyric poet Sappho, and she wore a crown, like Aphrodite, the goddess of love. Depending on the wedding budget, the ornament could be anything from a crown of fresh asparagus to an elaborate gold wreath, called a stephane. The design was a swirl of the leaves of the gods. Oak leaves from Zeus equaled strength. The ivy of Dionysus promised a great party. Apollo's laurel leaf twinkled with the spirit of perpetual youth. One or two cicadas perched on the branches symbolized the wedding songs. The stephane was worn with gold dangling earrings and an elaborate gold fringe necklace. A veil covered all the jewelry and the bride's face through the ceremony until the wedding feast, when she pulled it back.

In sixteenth-century i n d i a a bride did not receive an engagement ring, but she did get practically every other type of jewelry. Her family, friends, and fiancé gave gold and diamond or silver head ornaments, nose rings, necklaces, hand decorations, bangles, anklets, and toe rings as wedding presents. The jewels were symbols of a woman's married status, social standing, and religion (usually Hindu or Muslim), and also conveyed what part of India she came from. On the wedding day, in a splendid display of ornamental fireworks, everything was worn at once with a very vibrant red or pink dress.

High-society brides in **nineteenth-century england** received a diamond tiara as a wedding present from the groom or his family. It was an exquisite bit of required etiquette for married women in court circles to wear a tiara whenever they went to formal parties. On their wedding day, however, British brides chose to wear a tiara from their family's collection as tribute to their past. The rest of the bride's attire included a big, billowing white dress, glorious diamond earrings, a stunning necklace, and beautiful bracelets. The tiara towered above it all. It was the crowning glory of a bride's march down the aisle, an emblem of the happiness and dignity of a wedding.

Grace Kelly's engagement ring sparkled when she stopped for
photographers in New York City weeks before her 1956 royal wedding.

celebrity

STYLE

the glamour
and the glory

The fairy-tale romances of modern times are celebrity stories. Hollywood unions and royal weddings, these are the events that have set countless trends for contemporary brides. And jewelry is one of the most spectacular parts of the drama. It says a lot about the personal taste of the most beautiful and interesting brides in the world. An even closer look at the jewelry reveals intimate details of some epic love affairs.

With the ring on her finger, Marilyn Monroe and Joe DiMaggio kissed for the cameras right after their 1954 wedding.

THE RINGS

There is always talk of a honeymoon period, but a bride really begins to glow much earlier. In fact, it starts the moment she gets the proposal (naturally) and the ring. This is well documented with celebrity brides. When a star receives a glam rock, there is a change. Whether she shares every last detail with the press or denies the truth behind the ring on her left hand — she sparkles plenty. Suddenly she begins to talk with her hands, poses for photographs making her hands part of the picture, and dresses up a bit more, planning her looks in honor of the ring.

Grace Kelly puts her engagement ring in the MGM picture.

When Prince Rainier III of Monaco flew to America to propose to

grace kelly, he presented her with a Cartier eternity

band of rubies and diamonds, the colors of his country. On January 5, 1956,

at a press conference at Kelly's parents' home in Philadelphia, the happy

couple announced their engagement for newspapers, magazines, radio, and

newsreel cameras and let photographers take close-up pictures of the ring.

The engagement-ring story changed dramatically when the prince visited

the Oscar-winning actress in Los Angeles and saw the huge diamond

engagement rings movie stars were wearing.

Kelly displays her first
engagement ring from
Prince Rainier.

At home in Philadelphia with the prince, Kelly shows her mother, father, and the press her engagement ring.

He cabled Cartier in Paris immediately for a new ring. Kelly flaunted her second engagement ring, a 12-carat emerald-cut diamond flanked by two baguettes, in *High Society*. The ring was just right for her part as Tracy Lord, a Philadelphia society girl on the eve of her wedding. Kelly let the royal ring shine in MGM publicity stills, and when she posed for photographers outside her New York City apartment in March shortly before sailing to Monaco on the state-of-the-art luxury liner *Constitution,* which was making a special stop in the tiny principality just for her and her large wedding entourage.

The design of queen elizabeth's engagement ring was a royal family affair. Her creative suitor, Prince Philip, was given diamonds from his mother, Princess Andrew of Greece. His uncle, Earl Mountbatten of Burma, who liked to design jewelry for his wife, Edwina, recommended a good jeweler, the London firm Philip Antrobus Ltd. The engagement ring Philip conceived was a personal statement, not a flashy show of rank. It had a relatively small center stone for a future queen of England, a 3-carat round diamond, flanked by five smaller diamonds set in platinum. There was only one problem with the ring. On the big day, July 8, 1947, when he asked Elizabeth for her hand, the ring was too big to fit on her finger. In less than two days it was resized for the Buckingham Palace garden party at which the couple officially announced the engagement.

The official engagement photo
of Elizabeth and Philip.

When e l i z a b e t h   t a y l o r began to wear the 29.4-carat emerald-cut diamond engagement ring from legendary film producer Michael Todd at the end of 1956, she was in the process of divorcing her second husband, Michael Wilding, and claimed it was a "friendship ring." Todd told the press it was an engagement ring and joked, "It was not quite thirty but only twenty-nine-and-a-half carats." After the couple was happily married, on February 2, 1957, in Acapulco, Mexico, Taylor referred to the diamond frequently as "my ice skating rink."

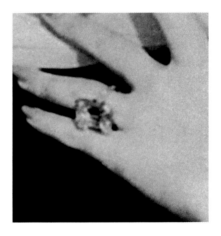

Eleanor Roosevelt (right) sails in her engagement ring.

Franklin Roosevelt proposed to e l e a n o r   r o o s e v e l t, his fifth cousin once removed, in the fall of 1903, when she was just nineteen years old. After she agreed to marry him, Roosevelt went shopping for a ring at Tiffany in New York City, where he was a Columbia Law School student. He examined several before choosing one with a 3.4-carat cushion-shaped diamond set in a gold ring with diamond and platinum details. Roosevelt gave the ring to his bride on her birthday, October 11, 1904. Enchanted by the jewel, Eleanor wrote Franklin a letter that night saying, "You could not have found a ring I would have liked better."

Roosevelt's ring.

"We are ours now 27 X 36" was the message King Edward VIII had engraved on the interior of the platinum engagement ring with a 19.77-carat rectangular emerald he gave Wallis Simpson. Edward proposed with the ring made by Cartier on October 27, 1936, a date that is the key to the inscription — 27 the day, X the month, and 36 the year. The date was

significant to the couple because it marked the beginning of Simpson's divorce proceedings from Ernest Simpson. When the prime minister, the press, and the public learned about the king's desire to marry an American woman soon to be twice divorced, it became a national crisis. The pressure was so intense the king decided to

The Duchess of Windsor's engagement ring.

abdicate. In his radio address to the nation on December 11, 1936, he said, "I have found it impossible to carry the heavy burden of responsibility and to discharge my duties as king as I would wish to do without the help and support of the woman I love." To celebrate their twentieth anniversary Wallis Simpson, who became the duchess of windsor when they married, had Cartier remount the ring into an elaborate gold-and-platinum design, but she kept the original mounting with its historic inscription all her life.

The Duchess of Windsor poses in her engagement ring on
December 3, 1936, seven days before Edward VIII abdicated.

After dating for two years, m a r i l y n m o n r o e
and Joe DiMaggio quickly decided to get married. The Yankee Clipper proposed
to his blonde bombshell on January 12, 1954. Two days later they went to City
Hall in San Francisco for what was supposed to be a secret civil ceremony with
six guests, but it was leaked to the press and one hundred photographers,
reporters, and fans showed up. Monroe wore a
simple chocolate suit with an ermine
collar and DiMaggio was in a dark
blue suit and the same tie he had
worn on their first date. At the end
of the three-minute ceremony
DiMaggio slipped a platinum eternity
band with 36 baguette-cut diamonds on
his bride's left hand. The flashy jewel was an
engagement ring and wedding band all rolled up
into one for Monroe.

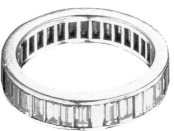

Monroe's engagement ring.

Monroe and DiMaggio
surrounded by newsmen as
they leave the courthouse
after their civil ceremony.

After a u d r e y h e p b u r n won the Oscar for *Roman Holiday* she traveled with her fiancé, Mel Ferrer, to Burgenstock, Switzerland, for some rest and relaxation followed by their wedding. Hepburn's svelte and stunning engagement ring was an eternity band of baguette-cut diamonds Ferrer bought from one of the most well respected jewelers in Europe, Gübelin of Zurich. On September 25, 1954, at a small chapel a short walk from their villa, the couple was married. During the ceremony Ferrer gave Hepburn two faceted wedding bands, one rose and one white gold. Understated and elegant, refined and original, the rings were a perfect expression of Hepburn's iconic style. She wore each separately, coordinating the delicate bands with outfits and occasions.

Hepburn's engagement ring and wedding bands.

Audrey Hepburn and Mel Ferrer.

The epic romance between Richard Burton and

e l i z a b e t h   t a y l o r

included two large and spectacular diamonds, the 33.19-carat Krupp and

the 69.42-carat Taylor-Burton. But neither of these gems was an engagement

ring. Instead he gave her an impressive emerald-and-diamond Bulgari

necklace (see page 70). When the couple was married on March 15, 1964,

Burton presented Taylor with a pavé-set diamond band. Days after the

wedding in Montreal they posed for photographers showing their rings.

He wore a gold signet-style ring.

An engagement photograph of John
and Jackie Kennedy in Hyannis Port.

j a c k i e   k e n n e d y teased her suitor, Senator John Kennedy, during their courtship through her newspaper column in the *Washington Times-Herald*. Once she wrote, "Can you give me any reason why a contented bachelor should ever get married?" Obviously the senator could. Right after she returned from covering Queen Elizabeth's 1953 coronation in London, he proposed with a Van Cleef & Arpels engagement ring. The crossover design featured a 2.84-carat emerald and a 2.88-carat diamond with baguette-cut diamond accents. When Jackie Kennedy became First Lady and famously redecorated the White House, she also had the ring redesigned, replacing the baguettes with marquise and round diamond accents.

The redesigned
Kennedy ring.

Kennedy's engagement
ring twinkled when she
celebrated her husband's
first-ballot victory for
the presidential nomination.

Frank Sinatra created a fireworks display on the Fourth of July weekend in 1966. He proposed to

mia farrow

with a 9-carat pear-shaped diamond and platinum engagement ring from Ruser, a mid-century Beverly Hills jeweler to the stars. When the engagement became public the *New York Post* headline read simply, "Sinatra Buys Mia the Ring." The couple was married in Las Vegas fifteen days later. A dazzling double-row diamond bracelet, also from Ruser, was one of the fifty-one-year-old Sinatra's wedding presents to his twenty-one-year-old bride.

Farrow hurries through the L.A. airport with a dog in one hand and
an engagement ring on the other four days before her Vegas wedding.

Prince Charles set a romantic scene with a candlelit dinner at Buckingham Palace to propose to lady diana spencer. He told her to take time and think it over, considering all the royal responsibilities that would come with marrying the future king of England. Diana accepted on the spot. At some point between the private dinner and the public announcement on February 24, 1981, Diana was shown a tray of rings from the British crown jeweler, Garrard. There are a few different theories on why she selected a sapphire instead of a diamond. Palace insiders have said the queen actually chose the $42,000, 18-carat oval sapphire surrounded by 14 diamonds. Some royal watchers believe Diana selected a sapphire because it matched her eyes. Diana herself was quoted as saying she picked her ring from the tray "because it was the biggest."

Hand in hand with rings.

Charles and Diana
announcing their
engagement.

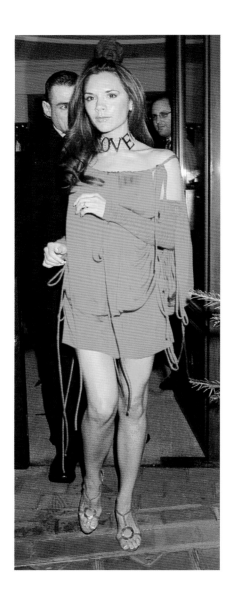

When V i c t o r i a   a d a m s,
otherwise known as Posh Spice from the late
nineties super girl group the Spice Girls, met
soccer star David Beckham in March 1997 after
one of his matches, it was love at first sight.
Beckham claims it was even earlier. He says he
found the girl of his dreams when he saw Adams
in the Spice Girls music video *Say You'll Be There*.
After ten months of dating, Becks popped the
question at the Rookery Hall Hotel in Cheshire,
England, with a 3-plus-carat marquise-shaped
diamond on a gold band from Manchester's jeweler

Victoria Beckham.

Boodle & Dunthorne. In a show of girl power, Adams gave her fiancé an engagement ring too. She asked Van Cleef & Arpels to make one of its women's gold and pavé-set diamond bands large enough for her athletic fiancé. The couple also exchanged matching gold Rolex watches to celebrate the occasion. Just over a year later, on July 4, 1999, Posh and Becks were married in a fifteenth-century Irish castle in Dublin.

David Beckham.

Posh and Becks modeled their rings and matching Rolexes for photographers when they announced their engagement.

When j a d a p i n k e t t and Will Smith decided to get married at the end of 1997, they went to the jeweler's together to pick out a ring. Their choice was a really large and glamorous pear-shaped diamond. "It is a big ol' ring," Pinkett told *Vogue*. "He wanted it bigger. A wife's ring is the core. I had to pick this one out, because I knew if I let Will pick it out I'd have had something like this" — referring to a sugar bowl. The couple was married on New Year's Eve in the bride's hometown of Baltimore.

During a Sting concert at the Beacon Theatre in New York City on November 21, 1999, Brad Pitt and jennifer aniston wowed the crowd with a song and a ring. Aniston showed off the diamond on her left hand while Pitt sang "Fill 'Er Up" with the lyrics: "We're going to Vegas, we're gonna get wed / So fill 'er up son, don't be staring / That's a real diamond she be wearing." After the public display of affection and jewelry the press was left to speculate on the engagement, which the couple would not confirm.

But it was indeed true. Pitt had been working for months with the Italian firm Damiani on the unique ring design. "Brad Pitt is inspired by art and architecture," says Silvia Damiani, who collaborated with the actor on the design. "He wanted the ring to be tactile and the stones to be set on different levels. The overall shape is related to the concept of a heart and it is a symbol of eternity."

The ring Brad Pitt
codesigned with Damiani.

In 1999, when Ryan Phillippe went to get actress

reese witherspoon

an engagement ring at Neil Lane, he chose a 4.5-carat Asscher-cut diamond

in a 1920s Art Deco setting. The ring was in perfect keeping with the couple's

appreciation for vintage things and old-fashioned ideas about

romance. Their courtship had

been filled with letters and

books, which they exchanged

when they were separated from

each other on location.

Witherspoon's attachment to her

ring — she posed in it for magazine

covers, and the diamond sparkled in

interviews — almost single-handedly

ignited the revival for Asscher cuts

in engagement rings.

On New Year's Eve in 1999 Michael Douglas proposed to his girlfriend of ten months, catherine zeta-jones, at his home in Aspen, Colorado. Douglas presented the raven-haired beauty with an absolutely magnificent ring from Fred Leighton featuring a vintage 10-carat marquise-shaped diamond set horizontally. "We have this case full of rings," remembered Leighton. "And Michael quickly narrowed the field down to two designs. Without knowing it he chose a ring Catherine had borrowed a couple of times for events. To me it meant they were made for each other."

jennifer lopez announced her engagement to Ben Affleck during ABC's *Primetime: Special Edition* interview with Diane Sawyer on November 13, 2002. Lopez told the story of the surprise proposal at Affleck's parents' house in Boston. "And he opens the door and it is just a blanket. A quilt of rose petals all over the whole, entire house. And just everything was just so, so many candles and vases with bouquets. And my song 'Glad' was playing." After

reading a love letter, he asked her to marry him and showed her a 6.1-carat radiant-cut fancy intense pink diamond with two trapezoid white diamond side stones mounted in platinum and 18K pink gold from Harry Winston. Her response: "But I didn't want to look at the ring because I could tell it was pink. And I was just like, oh, God, it can't be pink on top of it." Even though this ring never arrived at the altar—the couple canceled their September 14, 2003, wedding—the publicity surrounding it instantly created an international awareness and desire for rare pink diamonds.

Guy Ritchie decided to buy m a d o n n a a diamond ring immediately after she gave birth to their son, Rocco, in Los Angeles on August 11, 2000. On the recommendation of a friend, he went to Neil Lane, who specializes in vintage engagement rings, and chose a platinum Edwardian ring with three large diamonds. "He gravitated to the Edwardian style and all the history and detail being English," says Lane. When the press spotted the diamond sparkling from Madonna's left hand, she downplayed the jewel, saying simply, "It is a token of Guy's love and the fact that we just had a baby." The couple was married four months later.

Madonna's ring.

Madonna and Guy
Ritchie at the
January 2001
premiere of his
movie <u>Snatch,</u> in
their first public
appearance after
their super-private
wedding.

PRECIOUS WEDDING PRESENTS

When it comes to wedding presents, there are of course china, crystal, and silverware. For many celebrity brides there is also more jewelry — a lot more. Tiaras, big bracelets, necklaces, and complete sets with a necklace, earrings, bracelet, and ring, have added to the glamour of certain celebrity brides' engagement periods. Family and friends give jewelry, but usually it comes from the groom. Some famous fiancés have made jewelry a medium of their love, and their precious wedding presents are awesome.

Taylor's engagement brooch.

The emerald engagement brooch was Elizabeth Taylor's only jewel at her 1964 wedding to Richard Burton.

In 1962, when e l i z a b e t h   t a y l o r

and Richard Burton fell in love on the set of *Cleopatra* in Rome, they immediately began to celebrate their romance with extravagant jewelry. Shopping one afternoon at Bulgari, Burton bought Taylor an emerald, diamond, and platinum necklace. The pendant, an enormous 18.61-carat emerald surrounded by diamonds, could be detached and worn as a brooch. The necklace was Burton's first wedding present and proposal piece. In lieu of an engagement ring, she wore the brooch as often as possible, including onscreen in *The VIPs*. For the March 15, 1964, wedding, Elizabeth Taylor had Irene Sharaff, her costumer from *Cleopatra*, make a daffodil-yellow chiffon dress. The bright color was an arresting frame for the dazzling green of the engagement brooch Taylor pinned on her shoulder for the ceremony.

Taylor clipped her engagement brooch to her dress for a night on the town with Burton.

The Duke of Windsor gave Wallis Simpson a romantic, symbolic, and truly incredible bracelet as a wedding present. Going from the inside of the jewel out, the piece was inscribed: "For our Contract 18-V-37." It was the day, May 18, 1937, the couple's marriage contract was completed, the last obstacle they had to overcome before meeting at the altar. Van Cleef & Arpels in Paris made the bracelet in the shape of a garter, hence its name, Jarretiere, which means garter in French. The jewel was a sparkling play on a bride's garter and it covered the "something blue" category too, with a pool of cushion-shaped sapphires at the center of the wide diamond bracelet. The

duchess of windsor's

The Contract
Bracelet.

wedding dress, a blue satin crepe gown by

Mainbocher, was made to complement

the Contract Bracelet and another

wedding present from the duke, a

sapphire-and-diamond clip brooch.

The Duke and Duchess
of Windsor, photographed
by Cecil Beaton on their
wedding day.

Grace Kelly's
pearl-and-diamond
jewelry from
Prince Rainier.

Prince Rainier, friends, and several of Monaco's societies and citizens gave grace kelly jewelry as wedding presents. Monaco did not have a proper collection of crown jewelry, so the lavish gifts were necessary, required gear for the bride's future filled with official royal functions. Rainier went to his favorite jeweler, Van Cleef & Arpels, for several pearl-and-diamond pieces: a triple-strand necklace, a triple-strand bracelet with diamond blossoms, a pair of earrings, and a flower ring. The feminine jewels were not a matching set, but Kelly often wore them all together. Most of her other important presents came from Cartier in Paris, Kelly's favorite jeweler. The prince picked up a dazzling triple-tiered diamond necklace and the Société des Bains de Mer chose something every princess needs, a tiara. The delicate headgear featured diamonds and rubies, the red and white colors of Monaco. At the reception on the eve of her wedding, Kelly wore the necklace and tiara as well as a Cartier diamond bracelet, which was a wedding present from Aristotle Onassis.

Princess Diana in
Hong Kong in 1989.

l a d y   d i a n a received a treasury of precious wedding presents befitting her new position and the British royal family's legendary collection of historic pieces and giant gemstones. To name just a few: diamond pendant earrings from Prince Charles, a sapphire brooch from the Queen Mother, and an emerald-and-diamond choker from the queen. Among all the jewelry, the Cambridge Lover's Knot Tiara, also from the queen, was the most impressive. The headgear, made in 1914 by Garrard for Queen Mary, had nineteen pear-shaped oriental pearl drops and a significant number of diamonds. Inspired by a popular nineteenth-century design with diamond ribbons and floating pearls, the tiara was as feminine as it was majestic. Diana made it her traveling show-piece, pairing it with white gowns for a very modern regal effect on several official trips.

The Cambridge
Lover's Knot Tiara.

WEDDING DAY JEWELRY

Something old, something new, something borrowed, and something blue is one of the bride's formulas for good luck on her day of days. When part of the formula is taken care of with jewelry, as many celebrity brides choose to do, the results can be stunning. Old and borrowed turns into a magnificent historical display of pomp and circumstance when the bride is royal and she chooses a family treasure. In the case of some famous brides, jewelry is a pure fashion statement borrowed from their favorite jeweler. New jewelry worn down the aisle shows a bride's modern style and gives the public a peek at a celebrity couple's tokens of affection.

There were a series of jewelry mishaps before p r i n c e s s
e l i z a b e t h walked down the aisle on November 20, 1947,

to marry Prince Philip. The dazzling Russian fringe tiara she borrowed from

her mother popped off its frame when she was getting dressed at Buckingham

Palace. The court jeweler in attendance needed a police escort back to his

workroom to repair it quickly. Next, her wedding gift from her father, King

George VI — the historic Queen Anne and Queen Caroline pearl necklaces —

The Russian fringe tiara.

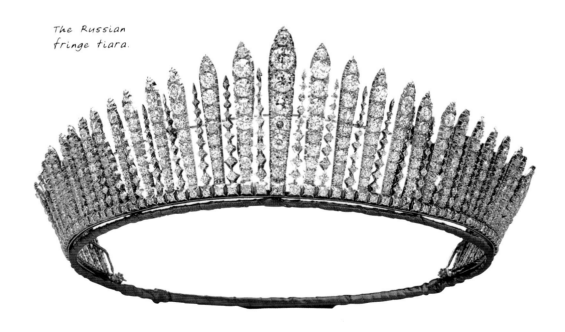

could not be found. The jewels, which matched the pearls embroidered on her satin wedding dress, were quickly located at St. James's Palace, where they were on exhibition with the rest of the wedding presents. With a half hour to spare before the carriage procession to Westminster Abbey, the princess's private secretary raced against time to get the pearls. Elizabeth miraculously made it to the church on time with every royal jewel in place.

Elizabeth and Philip in the royal coach after their wedding.

j a c k i e　k e n n e d y made sentimental jewelry choices for her wedding on September 12, 1953, at St. Mary's Church in Newport, Rhode Island. Her diamond bracelet was a wedding gift from John Kennedy. The diamond brooch she pinned to the neckline of her dress was another wedding present, this one from her favorite member of the Kennedy clan, her father-in-law-to-be, Joseph P. Kennedy. The delicate pearl choker was a borrowed piece from her side of the family.

When g r a c e k e l l y married Prince Rainier in Monaco on April 19, 1956, it was like a flawless Hollywood production. Jimmy Stewart, Cary Grant, Ava Gardner, and many other stars were there as guests, and the MGM cameras covered every second. Kelly walked down the aisle of the Cathedral of St. Nicholas in a gown of ivory silk taffeta and 125-year-old lace. Because of all the intricate lace — three hundred yards total — Kelly kept her jewelry very simple. She wore a favorite pair of double pearl earrings — the same jewels she had worn to the Oscars one month before the wedding.

Three-quarters of a billion people in seventy-four countries watched

lady diana marry Prince Charles at St. Paul's Cathedral in

London on July 29, 1981. For the big event the bride wore a gown made with

forty yards of silk, with puffed sleeves and a twenty-five-foot-long train. The

Spencer diamond tiara anchored her veil. Garrard designed the titled jewel

in 1937 around a nineteenth-century family brooch with scrolls and a floral

pattern. The tiara, which Diana paired with diamond pendant earrings,

became world famous after the wedding.

The Spencer tiara.

Diana and Charles in
the royal coach
after their wedding.

caroline kennedy

borrowed earrings from her mother for her July 19, 1986, wedding to
Edwin Schlossberg in a church near the Kennedy compound in Hyannis
Port. The earrings were designed in 1965 by one of Jackie Kennedy's
favorite jewelry designers, Jean Schlumberger, who worked exclusively
for Tiffany & Co. They exemplify Schlumberger's
creative style, with night-and-day, black
and white pearls and three sculptural
curling diamond leaves with gold veins.
The leaves loosely matched the luck-of-
the-Irish shamrock appliqués on her silk
organza Carolina Herrera dress.

Brad Pitt put a lot of effort into the smallest but most important jewels of a wedding, the wedding bands. He codesigned with Silvia Damiani the symbolic rings he and j e n n i f e r   a n i s t o n exchanged at their July 29, 2000, wedding in Malibu, California. A minimalist design, each ring featured two bands, one inside the other, joined by several little diamonds. "The rings reflected the modern concept of a couple," explains Damiani. "They maintain their individual identity but they are together." The subtlety of the diamonds in the design also matched the contemporary style of the bride and groom, harmonizing beautifully with the couple's cool wedding day clothes. Aniston walked down the aisle in a Lawrence Steel glass-beaded long silk-and-satin halter dress, and Pitt wore a Hedi Slimane tuxedo.

The rings provided all the usual drama during the exchange of vows as well as a bit of comedy. Pitt's best man, his brother, Doug, dropped one at the crucial moment.

The wedding bands Brad Pitt codesigned with Damiani.

m a d o n n a and Guy Ritchie's wedding on December 22, 2000, at cozy nineteenth-century Skibo Castle in Scotland was filled with old-world pageantry. The groom wore a traditional kilt and a blazer, and the bride walked down the aisle in a nineteenth-century–style ivory silk gown designed by Stella McCartney with a fitted corset top and a long train. Madonna had three amazing pieces of jewelry for the big event: an Edwardian diamond tiara, an extra-wide pearl-and-diamond bracelet, and a custom-made 37-carat diamond cross from Harry Winston.

The Winston cross
Madonna borrowed
for her wedding.

On November 18, 2000, catherine zeta-jones and Michael Douglas had an elegant black-tie wedding at New York's Plaza Hotel, attended by a star-studded list of 350 guests, including, of course, the groom's famous father, Kirk Douglas, as well as Goldie Hawn, Jack Nicholson, Danny DeVito, Meg Ryan, Russell Crowe, and Art Garfunkel, who performed. Zeta-Jones glowed in a white satin Christian Lacroix wedding dress and a dazzling nineteenth-century English diamond tiara from Fred Leighton. The majestic jewel, decorated with a pattern of swirling garlands, was fitting for the actress's marriage into a royal Hollywood family. The accessory was also a subtle nod to her beloved home in Wales. In the British Isles a diamond tiara has long been a symbol of the happiness and dignity of a wedding.

The Fred Leighton tiara Catherine Zeta-Jones borrowed for her wedding.

There were two stops on gwen stefani and Gavin Rossdale's wedding tour. The rock-and-roll couple was first married on September 14, 2002, in the groom's hometown, London. Two weeks later they had a second wedding, in the bride's hometown, Los Angeles. At both Stefani wore the same dress, custom-made by John Galliano of white silk with hot pink around the bottom and an antique lace veil. Five vintage diamond clips and barrettes from Fred Leighton accented her swept-up hair. The one costume change Stefani made between London and Los Angeles was her necklace. In London she had a delicate diamond cross and in Los Angeles she sparkled in a Georgian heart pendant of pink tourmalines, peridots, and diamonds set in silver and gold, suspended from a pink silk cord from Neil Lane. "She borrowed the necklace for a music video from the *Rock Steady* album and requested it for her wedding," says Lane. "She had the piece in London, but I think she saved it to make a special statement for her wedding at home in Los Angeles."

Rossdale gives Stefani the first bite of cake.

The Georgian heart pendant.

Diamond hair clips.

Stefani at her Los Angeles wedding.

your
STYLE

diamond rings
and other things

Details. Details. Details. There are a million details a couple has to handle as soon as they decide to get married. And the very first one, the purchase of an engagement ring, is probably the biggest of them all. It is like being thrown into the deep end of the pool. After that, in terms of jewelry, there is the possibility of a precious wedding present and the wedding day jewels. Every piece should be a perfect reflection of the bride's style. Remember, long after the cake has been eaten, the flowers have faded, and the dress has been put in storage, she will be wearing her engagement ring and wedding jewelry. And the bride — and groom — will want to live happily ever after with whatever they choose.

a ring glossary

The design of an engagement ring is purely a question of the bride's style. Is it classic, casual, glamorous, artistic, modern, or somewhere in between? The ring should blend naturally with the things she likes to wear and do. There are a few key design terms jewelers will use to describe the parts of a ring.

A round brilliant is at the center of a pavé-set pink diamond bypass ring by Chanel.

Bezel, or **Collet, Setting** Interchangeable terms, bezel and collet settings have a band of metal around the girdle of the gem.

Center Stone The largest stone at the center of a ring.

Channel Setting A band of square or baguette-shaped stones — all of equal size — set between two parallel rows of metal.

Crossover Ring or **Bypass Ring** The shank has a higher and lower arm that extend a little bit beyond the center. A gem can be set directly between the parts or at the end of each arm.

Micro Pavé Tiny diamonds pavéd across a metal surface.

Millegrain A decoration of very small platinum beads. Millegrain is an old technique found on rings from the 1890s to around 1920. Contemporary jewelers use millegrain on engagement rings to give them a vintage veneer.

Pavé Gems set as close together as possible across a metal surface.

Prong Setting Little metal claws that hold a gem in place.

Setting How a gem is mounted; for example, a prong setting or pavé setting.

Shank The band of a ring.

Shoulders The area of the side stones.

Side Stones The small stones flanking a center stone on an engagement ring. Most popular side stones are named for their shape — such as trapezoid, trillion (a triangular shape), and half-moon — except the baguette (a slender rectangular shape), which is named after the famous French bread.

Solitaire By definition a solitaire is a ring with one diamond, but the term is used loosely to refer to all engagement rings with a diamond center stone, even if it has side stones or other gem embellishments.

Split Shank A band that has two parallel lines or that splits into two or three parts, like a V or a W, at the sides of the center stone.

Tension Setting A shank that works as a clamp on the diamond and holds it in place. There is nothing, no prongs or anything else, between the shank and the stone.

Three Stone A ring with three stones of the same shape. They can be all the same size or a large center stone with slightly smaller side stones.

V-Tip A metal prong in the shape of a V, made to hold the ends of pear- or marquise-shaped diamonds.

A three-stone diamond ring by Cartier.

engagement rings

An engagement ring is the official symbol that wedding bells will soon be ringing. Facing the music and buying one, however, can be daunting. It takes time, money, design choices, and some knowledge of gemology. The most intense study is required for couples who want a ring with a diamond solitaire. Those looking for something simpler, like an eternity band, or a splash of color with a sapphire should also research the available options. The information in this section will give you the knowledge to make the perfect purchase. It will also make the experience more enjoyable and less intimidating.

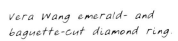

Vera Wang emerald- and baguette-cut diamond ring.

all about diamonds

A diamond engagement ring is the most expensive piece of jewelry most people will ever buy. A ring with a diamond of a carat or more can cost as much as a car or even a house. Yet compared to the purchase of these other big-ticket items, buying a diamond engagement ring is a relatively new experience for practically everyone. The majority of grooms, and indeed brides, only begin to look seriously at rings when they are planning to tie the knot. And once they begin to shop for a ring, it can be like traveling to a foreign country where people speak another language.

Vera Wang Asscher diamond and gold ring.

a diamond glossary

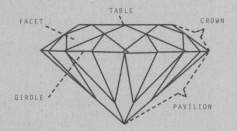

FACET · TABLE · CROWN · GIRDLE · PAVILION

Brilliance Light reflected through the crown. Cut is foremost, but color and clarity are also characteristics linked to a gem's brilliance.

Brilliant Facets Kite-shaped and triangular facets.

Crown The section of the stone above the girdle.

Dispersion The internal fireworks of a diamond, dispersion is technically the breakup of white light into rainbow colors. This magical feature cannot be captured on film. It is the life of the gem.

Gem Grading Reports Gem reports are a gemologist's review of quality with graphs and letter grades evaluating the 4Cs (see page 122). One of the well-respected gem grading reports comes from the Gemological Institute of America (GIA). Some fine jewelry firms such as Tiffany & Co. issue their own diamond certificates. If a jeweler does not show a couple a report for the stone they are planning to buy, they might consider going elsewhere.

Girdle A narrow band of facets separating the crown from the pavilion.

Facet The small planar surfaces of a cut diamond.

Fancy Color Diamonds Colored diamonds, such as pink and yellow.

Fancy Cut An umbrella term used for all diamond shapes except the round brilliant cut.

Fire The lively light of a diamond. Fire is a synonym for dispersion.

Flawless A diamond that shows no internal or external imperfections under a 10-power jeweler's loupe.

Inclusion Any internal flaw.

Mixed and **Modified Cuts** Some diamonds are not textbook examples of a shape. Stones with brilliant-style facets, say, and a few step cuts are called mixed cut. Modified cut is used to refer to gems with more or fewer facets than the classic round brilliant cut. A mixed or modified cut is not a sign of lesser quality. These unique stones are often highly coveted for their originality.

Octahedron An eight-sided solid, resembling two pyramids joined at the base; the natural form of most diamond crystals.

Pavilion The section of the stone below the girdle.

Rough An uncut diamond.

Spread An extra-large table, usually more than 60 percent of the crown.

Step Cuts Long slender facets, step cuts usually appear in threes going up crowns and down pavilions like stairs.

Stone Papers Sheets of special jeweler's paper, folded into little packets to hold a diamond. The gem's carat weight, color, and clarity grade are generally written on the outside. A couple will see stone papers if they choose a diamond before it is put into a setting — a common practice with engagement rings.

Table The largest facet on top of the stone, parallel to the girdle.

metal matters

There are two types of metals used on engagement rings: platinum and gold. Each one has unique properties.

- **Platinum,** the most expensive and rare metal, is the strongest. It is the most impervious to hard knocks and scratches. For prongs, it is unbeatable. Platinum holds a white diamond securely and sets off the color perfectly. Rings with yellow gold shanks frequently have platinum prongs or a platinum collet setting for practical and aesthetic reasons.

A diamond-and-platinum ring by R. Esmerian.

- **Gold** comes in several colors, including yellow, white, and pink. Yellow has been used in diamond engagement rings for hundreds of years. The sunshine metal makes a warm design. When yellow gold is used on prongs or a collet setting it can cast a very faint yellow light over a white diamond. To match the hue of pink and yellow diamonds, pink and yellow gold are used on the prongs and collet, if not on the entire ring. White gold looks a lot like platinum, but it is a little less expensive and not quite as strong.

A diamond-and-gold ring by Bulgari.

start with shape

Square-cut or pear-shape,
these rocks don't lose their shape.

—"Diamonds Are a Girl's Best Friend"

The best way to approach the purchase of a diamond engagement ring is by breaking it down into parts. A good starting point is the shape of the stone. There are many different diamond shapes available, each with its own history and character. It is important to analyze the options. A round brilliant, a cushion, an Asscher, or any of the other many diamond shapes will be the star of the ring.

The classic Tiffany Setting has six prongs holding a round brilliant above a slender band.

ROUND BRILLIANT

Far and away the most popular diamond shape for engagement rings is the round brilliant. Designed by Marcel Tolkowsky in 1919, the round brilliant has an ingenious arrangement of fifty-eight facets, which cause the light beams to bounce from the pavilion back through the crown. Previously, round diamonds lost light through the bottom of the stone. On top of its great light, the shape is really versatile in designs. The round brilliant looks classic in simple settings and blends harmoniously with elaborate rings.

Above and left: Harry Winston's glamorous ducktail setting, launched around 1947, displays a round brilliant flanked by tapered baguettes. The shank sweeps in below the side stones, like a ducktail. From the top all you see is diamonds.

A diamond ribbon
wraps around a round
brilliant on an ultra-
feminine Dior ring.

The sweet Gumdrop
ring with a round
brilliant by Chris
Correia has a curvy
band with diamond
sprinkles.

A delicate design,
Michael B's ring
combines a round
brilliant with a
narrow pavé-set
diamond band.

A graceful leaf of
pavé-set diamonds
curls from one end
of a round brilliant
to the other in a
Van Cleef & Arpels
Acanthus ring.

A round brilliant sits
in a collet on top of
a stylish diamond
split-shank ring
by H. Stern.

A sporty white gold band by Suzanne Felsen has a round brilliant at the center with diamond studs above and below.

The arty platinum Omega ring by Steven Kretchmer clamps a round brilliant in a tension setting.

A round brilliant tops a bold gold link ring by Verdura.

A cool wide gold band by Tiffany holds a round brilliant in a demicollet setting.

Old-world elegance characterizes Temple St. Clair Carr's gold ring with a round brilliant.

PEAR

A pear luxuriates in the totally contemporary lines of a De Beers ring.

The lopsided, voluptuous, and feminine pear has played a starring role in jewelry since at least the eighteenth century, when pear-shaped stones were called *pendeloques* and used as pendants in diamond necklaces and chandelier earrings. They are one of the most difficult shapes for lapidaries to cut because of their unusual form. In fact, some say the art of diamond cutting is best expressed in a large, luscious, contemporary pear with fifty-six to fifty-eight facets.

Pears are delicious in rings with garnishes. Be aware that with the pear, it is difficult to find a wedding band that fits perfectly underneath the rump of the stone. Some engagement rings lift the stone a bit above the finger so a wedding band can snuggle up next to it. If the ring is not designed to accommodate a wedding band, a couple can have one specially made with a curve in the center, or a bride can wear her pear solo.

PRINCESS

The princess is a flirty, flashy shape. Designed in 1961 by Arpad Nagy in London, it has a big flat crown, a square girdle, and anywhere from 49 to 144 facets. There is a hall-of-mirrors effect to the faceting that can hide many imperfections in color and clarity. The corners of the princess are sharp and should be protected in a ring setting with prongs to prevent chipping. Bold and beautiful engagement rings are best for the extrovert shape. The dazzling princess is made in heaven for eternity bands because the edges line up and create a solid wall of gems.

An audacious De Beers ring has a princess center stone on a wide baguette-cut diamond band.

how to keep your ice nice

- Diamond rings get dirty easily, but they are simple to clean. Bathe the ring in a little warm water with mild soap once a week. Air-dry it on a paper towel and then polish it with a soft cloth.

- At least once every two years try to take the ring back to the jeweler for a good steam or ultrasonic cleaning and a checkup to make sure the prongs around the diamond are secure.

- Diamonds are one of the strongest materials on earth, but they can scratch. When it is not out and about, let the ring rest in its own special box or pouch.

Two trillion side stones attend a princess in a confident H. Stern ring.

One large and two
smaller emerald-cuts
make a striking Kwiat
three-stone ring.

EMERALD

No shape more aptly fits the diamond
nickname "ice" than the emerald cut.
Developed in the Art Deco era, the
emerald cut has long, glamorous lines
defined by a rectangular table, numer-
ous step-cut facets down the crown
and pavilion, and diagonally cut corners on the girdle. The large table
shows off clarity better than any other
shape. Its confusing name was taken
from the most popular shape for
emeralds in the 1920s. Emerald-cuts
shine in designs with clean lines.

A stunning Winston ring
showcases an emerald-
cut and tapered
baguettes.

Sleek tapered
baguettes hug an
emerald-cut in a
Scott Kay ring.

ROSE

The exotic rose has a round girdle, flat bottom, and domed crown covered with triangular facets. Sometimes the facets rise to a point on top like a Hershey candy kiss. Sometimes there is a small table. Invented during the fifteenth century in India, roses were popular in Europe until the eighteenth-century invention of the cushion. The pretty floral shape began to blossom again around 2000 in engagement rings.

Unique and chic, an
R. Esmerian ring has a
row of fresh rose-cuts.

MARQUISE

The marquise diamond is noble to the core. Legend has it that the shape — a ship shape really, with rounded sides and a point at each end — was invented during the eighteenth-century reign of Louis XV. Supposedly, it was named in honor of the French king's mistress, the Marquise de Pompadour. Another version of the story ties the shape to the marquise-shaped rings worn by courtiers at Versailles to flaunt their rank. Contemporary marquise-cuts have a hexagon-shaped table, thirty-two trapezoid and triangular facets on the crown, and twenty-four facets on the pavilion. Vintage-style rings are the greatest compliment to the old-world grace of marquise diamonds.

Round diamonds surround a marquise in a charming Smithwick-Dillion ring.

A marquise is set as a grand horizontal in a Fred Leighton pavé-set diamond ring.

ASSCHER

The Asscher is a striking and dramatic square. Designed around 1902 by Abraham Asscher of the famous diamond-cutting Asschers of Amsterdam, it has a high crown with a small table, large step cuts, cut corners on the girdle, and a deep pavilion. The shape — considered one of the first modern shapes and a forerunner of the emerald cut — enjoyed a period of popularity from its invention to around 1930. The Asscher came back into vogue in the late 1990s. Gem cutters, including the Asschers, began to make modern variations on the earlier style. The difference between the old and the new is mainly around the table. Older Asschers have a small table and shimmering light. Modern versions

A beautiful Art Deco-style diamond ring by Neil Lane is set with an Asscher.

A dazzling Asscher is the center stone of an Edwardian-style Neil Lane ring.

have a larger table and more brilliance. Geometric Art Deco and frilly Edwardian-style engagement rings work best with the Asscher.

CUSHION

The cushion delivers sophistication and elegance. In the age of candlelight — that is, the eighteenth and nineteenth centuries — the square shape with curved sides and rounded corners shone softly. In the early twentieth century the shape disappeared with the excitement over the bright round brilliant. Cushions made a big comeback as a refined, ladylike shape for engagement rings in the late 1990s with the renewed appreciation for vintage jewelry.

The grand cushion of Martin Katz's micro-pavé-set diamond ring rests in micro-pavé diamond prongs.

Spectacular, spectacular describes the view from the top of a Fred Leighton ring with an ample cushion in a micro-pavé diamond collet setting. A side view reveals a superslender micro-pavé band rising up along the sides of the pavilion of the big cushion.

ASHOKA

The exquisite Ashoka is a new-old diamond shape. Launched in 1999 by William Goldberg, the shape is based on one legendary diamond named after the Buddhist warrior-king Ashoka (ca. 265–238 B.C.), whose name means the power to remove sorrow. When exactly the Ashoka was first cut no one knows for sure. A good guess would be the eighteenth century. The Ashoka was a variation on the cushion, the most popular shape of the era. The new Ashoka features a rectangular outline and sixty-two facets. "It has a unique fire and brilliance of its own," explains Goldberg. "It is soft." The beautiful Ashoka faceting stands out in simple rings and looks elegant in neovintage designs.

A gorgeous William Goldberg Ashoka ring is encrusted with diamonds.

A minimalist William Goldberg ring has one horizontally set Ashoka.

A triple split shank
pavéd in diamonds adds
extra flash to Stephen
Russell's oval-cut
diamond ring.

OVAL

The oval is an artistic cousin of the
round brilliant. It reflects light almost
as dramatically, with fifty-eight facets.
Historically the oval was used mainly
for rubies and sapphires, which are
easier to cut than diamonds. When
gem-cutting techniques improved in
the twentieth century, more diamonds
were made into ovals. Like the round
brilliant, the oval fits beautifully in
both minimal- and maximal-style
engagement rings.

A ladylike Cartier ring
has an oval with a few
diamonds on either side.

LUCIDA

Tiffany's Lucida diamond was
launched in 1999. Its name comes
from the term used to designate the
brightest star in a given constellation
or group of stars. It is a graceful
square with wide corners and
forty-nine or fifty facets. The firm's
first ring for the Lucida was a stream-
lined design made to show off the fine
features of the shape. This idea of a
setting created especially to turn on
the lights of a gem, so to speak, is
reminiscent of Tiffany's 1886 revolu-
tionary prong setting for the
round brilliant.

Modern and magnificent,
the Tiffany Lucida ring
perfectly complements the
geometry of the gem.

DESIGNER SHAPES

David Yurman ring.

Movado ring.

The heart, soul, and star of an engagement ring is the center stone. For jewelry designers who want to make an engagement ring a total expression of their style, the logical next step has been to design the shape of the diamond. The concept is relatively new. It began around 1998 with designers reinterpreting and modernizing classic cuts, like the round brilliant or the cushion.

The debutante diamonds are sometimes named after the jeweler who made them, like David Yurman's DY cut or the Movado diamond. Other times the names are romantic, such as the Ashoka or Lucida. More often than not, these diamonds are patented to maintain exclusivity to the designer.

NEW VS. OLD DIAMOND SHAPES: choose your fire

The fire and brilliance of every diamond shape is a little different. There is a definite divide, however, between the new and old diamond cuts. (Generally speaking, new with diamonds refers to shapes cut after the 1919 round brilliant.) A bright, intense, electric light goes off in a well-cut modern stone, with the round brilliant leading the light brigade. Old diamond shapes like Asschers, roses, and cushions have a soft, candlelike light. The new versions of these old shapes are brighter than their antique counterparts but not quite the high voltage of the real moderns. Which is better? Each has a unique personality, whether strong or subtle. The beauty contest is judged in the eye of the beholder.

An antique rose-cut diamond ring by Renee Lewis.

A modern Asscher-cut diamond ring by Daniel K.

learn the 4Cs

Once a couple has a general idea about the shape, it is time to start looking deeply into the stone and learning to speak the language of diamonds, otherwise known as the 4Cs: carat weight, clarity, cut, and color. Being familiar with the terms will make shopping for gems much easier. And it will clarify the one-page grading report that every gem of 1 carat or more should have. Above all else, understanding the 4Cs will demystify the price of a diamond, which accounts for about 85 percent of the price of an engagement ring. Many people believe the value of a diamond is based solely on carat weight. This is not true. It is a combination of all the 4Cs. And there are many ways to work the numbers based on these factors. Diamonds of the same carat weight may not be of equal value because of variations in color, cut, or clarity. Take time to study the variables and find out which of the 4Cs means the most to you both.

CARAT WEIGHT

The size of a diamond is measured in carat weight. This practice of weighing a stone, as opposed to, say, measuring its height, width, and depth, goes back to ancient times, when diamonds were weighed in a scale with the more or less uniform seeds of a carob tree. The word carat comes from keration, the Greek word for a carob tree.

The measurement for gems was standardized in 1913 in the United States by fixing the weight of 1 carat at 200 milligrams. Fractions of a carat are divided into points, and there are 100 points in a carat. So a 1½ carat stone, for example, is referred to as a 1.5-carat diamond. Diamonds of less than 1 carat, such as side stones of an engagement ring, are sometimes called pointers. A half-carat diamond is a 50-point stone.

On average, diamond engagement rings are from 1 to 3 carats. You will pay a lot more for round numbers like 1, 2, or 3 carats. If you choose a stone that is just short of these numbers, you can save significantly. Keep in mind when you are looking at diamonds that every shape carries its weight differently. The bulk of a round brilliant is on top, like an umbrella, where you can see it. An Asscher hides a lot of weight in the pavilion. The deep bottom makes it look smaller than other square and rectangular shapes with a more even distribution of weight.

CLARITY

Paradoxically, the term clarity is mainly used to refer to the flaws in a diamond. Gems with no inclusions, or superficial blemishes, are called flawless (FL) or internally flawless (IF) and are extremely rare. Most gems have a flaw of some sort, called by such names as crystal, pinpoint, or feather. The level of flaws — their number and visibility — is graded by a gemologist and expressed in letters and numbers. VVS1 and VVS2 are grades for very, very slightly included diamonds. VVS2 diamonds have fractionally more inclusions than VVS1. VS1 and VS2 are very slightly included gems. Diamonds with a V in the clarity grade are good stones. The flaws in these grades — with the occasional exception of a VS2 — can only be seen under the 10-powered magnification of a jeweler's loupe. Diamonds graded SI1 and SI2 for slightly included and I1, I2, and I3 for included are stones with obvious inclusions. These are not quality stones.

A pink and white diamond bypass ring by Martin Katz.

CUT

The term cut is used in several ways. In 4Cs lingo, cut refers to the facet arrangement on the surface of the gem. Brilliance pervades a well-cut diamond. Brilliance fades when the cutter leaves a stone's flaws intact and trims the facets badly in an effort to maintain carat weight.

Cut is also a synonym for shape. Sometimes it is linked with certain shapes as part of their name, such as the round brilliant cut or an emerald cut. It is correct to say the shape is a round brilliant or it is a round brilliant cut.

COLOR

When used in relation to white diamonds, the term color actually refers to the absence of color. The best white diamonds are colorless or nearly so, without any tints of yellow or brown. The color grading scale begins with D, the best colorless stone, and ends with Z. Good stones range from D through I.

A jump in grade from one letter to the next can mean a difference of thousands of dollars in the price. If you are wondering why the scale begins with D, it is because it replaced a grading scheme with three rungs: AAA, AA, and A. In 1957 the diamond industry started using the new scale, which began with D to prevent any confusion with the old system.

On the opposite end of the spectrum, so to speak, yellow and pink diamonds have their own grades. Adjectives are used to describe the degree of color, otherwise known as saturation. Highly saturated stones are called fancy vivid and then, moving down the scale, fancy deep, fancy intense, fancy, and fancy dark. Different from the white diamond grading system where a D is definitively better than an E, the color of a pink or yellow diamond is somewhat subjective. If you are interested in a soft cotton-candy pink, the highest color grade and the most expensive fancy vivid is probably too strong for your taste. To make matters more complicated, diamonds in the same color grade, say fancy intense, can have very small doses of modifying colors, giving them an entirely different look one from the other. Colored diamonds graded faint, very light, light, and fancy light are not considered quality grades for engagement rings. A diamond in these grades can provide a bride with a larger stone for less money. It is something to consider for people who are purely interested in carat weight, not real color.

A yellow and white diamond ring by Tiffany.

pink and
yellow diamonds

Pink and yellow diamond engagement rings are very sweet and truly special, not to mention very rare and truly expensive, much more so than white diamond engagement rings. Sure, they have innocent good looks. But don't be fooled, they are worldly gems. Finding a hue that is just right for you can be difficult. Even the finest jeweler might need some time to resource the perfect cotton-candy pink, for example. Because of these challenges, fancy colored diamonds are unique in engagement rings. Yellow diamonds, nicknamed canaries, are the more common of the two pastels. They started appearing on the third finger of the left hand in the 1980s. Pink diamonds came into engagement ring vogue after a certain celebrity received her 6.1-carat rock.

A pink and white diamond ring by Winston.

buying a diamond

A BRIDE'S-EYE VIEW

Abride whom we shall call Lisa (not to protect her identity but to keep peace with her fiancé) told us that she daydreams every once in a while about the diamond she didn't get. After weeks of diamond shopping she and her husband-to-be had narrowed the field to two oval-cut gems. According to the Gemological Institute of America's Diamond Grading Reports on the stones, one was a 2.34-carat, E color, VS1 clarity and the other a 3-carat, I color, VS1. In other words, the second stone was larger but the color was not as good (and incidentally it cost less). The couple settled on the smaller, higher-quality stone. Lisa admits, however, "I liked the larger diamond, and I couldn't see the difference between the two."

The GIA Diamond Grading Reports that guided their decision were the products of a grading system that has taken on a life of its own since it was introduced in 1956. Its purpose, then as now, was to protect consumers in the market for solitaires from fraud and to standardize diamond ratings. The report lays out the measurements and other physical characteristics of a diamond in a concise system of numbers, letters, and diagrams. Over the years this grading system has become the industry standard.

It is important to understand that the GIA report gives basic information about a diamond but is not an appraisal. To make this point clearly, at the bottom of the document is the disclaimer, "This report is not a guarantee, valuation, or appraisal." Nevertheless, the report exerts a tremendous influence on diamond buyers. It encourages them to purchase the higher-quality stones, which are more expensive. Some clients, knowing that a D flawless is the highest grade on a GIA report, will settle for nothing less.

The report can also instill a false sense of confidence that the information it contains is all one needs to make a purchase. Diamonds have

qualities that the report doesn't exactly report. "Certificates have their importance and play a substantial role, but it doesn't tell you about creativity and beauty," says jeweler Martin Katz. "There is a personality and sex appeal to diamonds, a life to the stones that doesn't show up on paper." In short, every diamond is unique — and the scientists at the GIA are quick to admit as much. "It is near impossible to catch the magic and beauty of a diamond by the information written in a GIA report," says GIA gemologist John King. "There's something important about using your eye as well. The eye is not meant to be replaced by the report."

Like our friend Lisa, most people cannot discern the difference between a D stone and an I, the lowest color grade for white diamonds. Why should anyone be expected to make such subtle distinctions when the difference between a D color grade and an I to the untrained eye is "probably small," according to King?

What you do see is the difference in the price. The individuality of each stone and the many possible combinations of the 4Cs make it impossible to create a standard price list. But a D, internally flawless, round brilliant–cut, 1 carat diamond costs approximately 30 percent more than an E and 50 percent more than an F diamond of the same clarity, weight, and cut.

So why pay dearly for the color of a diamond if you can't even see it? "Over time you will notice more about the diamond you wear on your hand every day," explains jeweler Fred Leighton. "And a good white diamond is always white, it never gets yellow." Second, good old-fashioned bragging rights are involved. "Egos are important, and what we tell our neighbors is important," says William Goldberg. "If you want to talk about your diamond, you should get a Mercedes stone." Finally, knowing you have a diamond with good color will give you a feeling of great confidence if you ever sell it or trade it in for an even better stone. Though our bride, Lisa, admits to missing the extra carat weight on her finger, she says all these reasons led her to choose the finer diamond.

trading up

An engagement ring celebrates one
milestone for everyone. Some people
use it to celebrate another. For a
significant anniversary, a big birthday,
or the birth of a child, they trade in
the center stone for a finer or larger
diamond and put it in a new setting.
If you think you might one day take
such a step — and even if you don't —
do ask when you are buying your ring
if the jeweler would accept the center
diamond (or the whole ring) as pay-
ment toward another stone or new
ring in the future. A fine jeweler will
say yes.

A Boucheron diamond ring.

engagement rings
SOME ALTERNATIVES

There is no official design for an engagement ring. Although the majority of brides have chosen a ring with a solitaire diamond for at least the last hundred years, it is not a requirement for getting engaged.

Brides and grooms can choose any type of ring they want to celebrate their engagement. A sapphire, an eternity band, or a symbolic design are a few alternative ideas.

Diamonds light up
the Comet bypass
ring by Chanel.

A sapphire adds a
splash of color to an
exotic gold-and-enamel
Sharon Alouf ring.

Rose-cut diamonds
accent the yellow and
oxidized white gold
floral Buccellati band.

A delicate nineteenth-century
ring from R. Esmerian has
a sapphire at the center of
a diamond square.

A sapphire design classic
from R. Esmerian features
a cushion-cut and diamond
side stones.

A little modern masterwork
by Van Cleef & Arpels
presents an oval sapphire
in a sleek wide ring with
two tracks of baguettes.

SAPPHIRES

Sapphires are the most popular gem choice for the small band of brides who leave the great white way of diamonds. The navy gem is eye-catching as well as being practical. It works easily with almost any wardrobe. Like diamonds, sapphires are judged on cut, color, and carat weight. One great advantage of the blue-ribbon stone is that they are frequently flawless. Where a sapphire comes from, the country of origin, also affects its value. Bright Burmese or Kashmir sapphires are rare and expensive. Whether they are heat treated or natural will affect the price too, natural being costlier. In a price per carat comparison, generally sapphires cost less than diamonds. The blue stone makes many types of rings — classic, vintage, exotic, and modern — a beautiful rhapsody in blue.

ETERNITY BANDS

Sleek and easy, eternity bands are an appealing alternate for modern brides. By loose definition — and there is only a loose definition — an eternity band is a band with gems, usually diamonds. They come in a range of styles, from a deluxe design with huge rocks all the way around to a band of gold sprinkled with a few diamonds. The style can be a great economizer. An eternity band set with small to medium-sized stones can cost fifty percent less than a ring with a 1-carat solitaire. It is also a bit of a no-brainer. You do not have to study the 4Cs to buy one of these. The diamonds are usually not large enough to require a gem certificate. If a bride chooses an eternity band as her only ring, before the wedding it is taken off and then put on again during the ceremony.

OGI

Tiffany

William Goldberg

Caroline Ellen

Penny Preville

Cartier

Cathy Waterman

Winston

Elsa Peretti

Me & Ro

Leslie Greene

OGI

Stephen Webster

Schlumberger

SYMBOLIC DESIGNS

Rings with things like stars, a tiara, or even a Catherine wheel for a whirlwind courtship, are ideas for brides looking for something different. They are also a great idea for brides looking for something less expensive. A ring without a diamond center stone, as a general rule, costs much less than a ring with a certified diamond. These joyous jewels can, of course, be worn every day, or they can be saved for special occasions. There is also no rule anywhere that says you have to wear your engagement ring all the time. Alternate your unusual design with a simple wedding band.

The Catherine Wheel Ring by Solange Azagury-Partridge.

The Tiara ring by Karen Karch for Push.

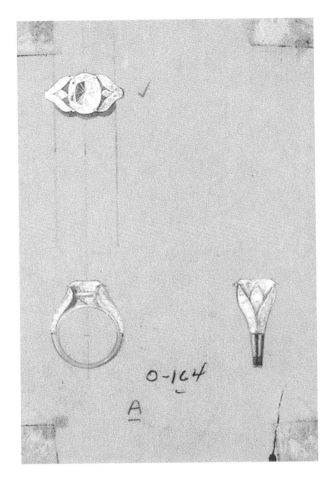

O-164

A

Verdura drawings.

#3   1350 -

designing your own engagement ring

It is out of the ordinary, and quite extraordinary, for someone to custom-design a necklace, earrings, or a bracelet with their favorite jeweler. When it comes to engagement rings, however, the idea of collaborating with a jewelry designer is common. How does it work?

The first step is to find a jeweler who has a style you like. Next comes the center stone. You may want to use a family gem. Or the jeweler will present you with a selection of gems to choose from. Then comes the building of the ring. This is not done entirely from scratch. You pick details from rings in the collection and go from there.

Some fine jewelers, like Bulgari or Verdura, for example, do a highly detailed drawing for the client to study and make alterations to. Bulgari includes the finished sketch, with the company seal watermark, in the package with the ring. Other designers, such as Me & Ro, will discuss ideas on style with a bride and groom. Next the couple reviews a silver version of

the ring. Finally, the design is made in gold or platinum and set with the gems.

Every jeweler approaches the couture process a little differently. Before getting started, ask how it is done. Ask what it costs — some jewelers don't charge extra, others have minimums. Also find out how long it takes. It is a process for patient couples. On average, jewelers require three months to build a brand-new ring.

Two Me & Ro rings.

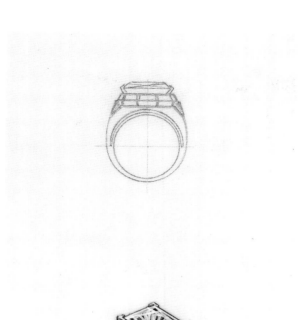

Bulgari drawings.

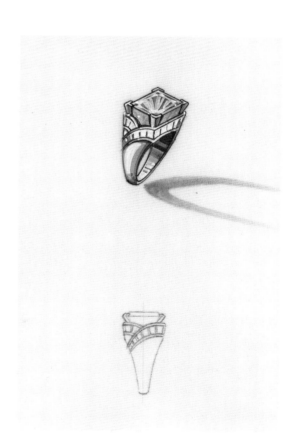

precious wedding presents

Becoming engaged is a major milestone. It is nice to celebrate the occasion with a precious wedding present, something that will last a lifetime and can be passed down through generations. In the immediate future, a fine accessory dresses up any ensemble, from casual to cocktail. Such accents make couples shine a little brighter on their special occasions — the engagement parties, bridal shower, bachelor party, family celebrations, rehearsal dinner, and so on — where they will be the hosts or guests of honor.

for the groom

A watch is the greatest accessory to give a groom. It has become a modern tradition for the bride to present one to her fiancé shortly after she receives the engagement ring. Choose a classic timepiece he can wear every day, one that dresses up casual clothes and looks just right at formal events. Be sure to engrave the back with a special message and perhaps the date of the wedding. The time symbolism can even be played out with a little joke — "Get to the church on time!" — or a sweet sentiment — "Love Forever."

for the bride

The best jewelry wedding present for a bride will complement her ring. Think diamonds. It is a perfect moment for her to receive a family jewel. For a new jewelry gift, choose a clean design that will withstand the trends of time. Diamond earrings, studs or hoops, are a great gift for a bride. They will light up her face in photos. A diamond line bracelet adds a flood of light to the engagement ring she will be showing off every day. The bracelet could also be the first in a collection assembled over special anniversaries. In the 1920s, line bracelets were nicknamed service stripes, given for every year of marriage. An alternative to jewelry is a wonderful watch, for busy brides who have so many appointments to keep before the wedding.

Diamond line bracelet.

Diamond studs.

Diamond hoops.

wedding day jewelry

The bride is the center of attention at any wedding. She is the one in the glorious dress and beautiful jewelry. To pull off the style of the starring role perfectly, she must always think of the two together. The dress is critical, of course, but the jewelry is equally important. Wedding day jewelry, which is almost always white — diamonds or pearls — will personalize and perfect a bride's appearance.

A bride should pick one focal point around her face for an impact piece: a pair of pendant earrings, a necklace, or a hair ornament. It is the jewel people will see when they look at her, and it will shine in photographs. Guests won't necessarily see the wedding bands exchanged during the vows, but these rings are as important as wedding day blockbusters. The couple will wear them every day as a symbol of their union.

wedding bands

Rarely are engagement rings and wedding bands purchased at the same time. Most couples wait until right before the big day to buy their wedding bands. For women and men alike, the bands are usually simple slender circles of gold or platinum. The plain pieces are personalized with engraving on the interior — the couple's initials, their names, or a poetic phrase. Every once in a while couples choose bands with a few flourishes. Wide bands with a motif around the center are one alternative choice for grooms. Slender diamond eternity bands are very popular with brides. Whatever the style, a wedding band should be in sync with every aspect of your life. While an engagement ring can be left at home for whatever reason, married people never go without their wedding bands.

Wedding bands.

M + J savitt pearl necklace.

necklaces

If a bride chooses a strapless dress, she absolutely should wear a necklace. She will look bare without one. The style should match the mood of the dress. A classic strapless and a pearl choker are a winning, can't-go-wrong combination. A relaxed bohemian strapless and a multi-strand gold necklace with small pearls are laid-back chic. An embroidered strapless dress and a simple diamond choker have a mighty sophisticated gleam. And a classic white column of satin and a diamond necklace with exquisite details are absolute elegance. Any necklace, from classic to bohemian, fills the expanse of empty real estate, becoming a glamorous bridge between the dress and the veil.

Elsa Peretti diamond necklace.

Van Cleef & Arpels pearl-
and-diamond necklace.

Winston diamond
pendant earrings.

earrings

I f a bride sweeps her hair in an up-do, as so many choose to, a pair of earrings are, as the French say, de rigueur. Her ears will look incomplete without at least a little stud. If earrings are to be the focal point of her jewelry, a pair of pendants is a good choice. Styles in pendant earrings begin with a twinkling drop and expand to full chandeliers. Small pendants should be paired with a beautifully embroidered or lacy frock. Chandeliers blaze with dramatically flowing dresses. Small or large, earrings bring it all together and make a great frame for the face.

Vintage-style pendant
earrings by Neil Lane.

Diamond Kwiat
star earrings.

Cynthia Bach diamond
chandelier earrings.

Renee Lewis diamond
Shake earrings.

Elara three-stone
tassel earrings.

Fred Leighton diamond
pendant earrings.

hair ornaments

A bride who wants to create a modern-day story-book look should wear diamonds in her hair. It is written in the script: a wedding is the one day that every bride is like royalty and has rights to a tiara. But instead of wearing that tiara in an old-fashioned way, she could consider combining a bandeau-style tiara, essentially a wide headband, and a sleek, chic gown. A bride who chooses to crown her attire with a dazzling headpiece should keep the other jewelry to beautiful basics like studs and a line bracelet and hold the necklace entirely. The rules change if instead of wearing a tiara a bride attaches a pretty clip or comb to her chignon. It will only be seen from behind and does not affect the way the rest of her jewelry is arranged. Accents at the back of the head just create all-around perfection.

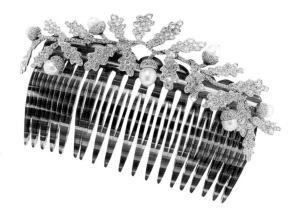

Fred Leighton
acorn comb.

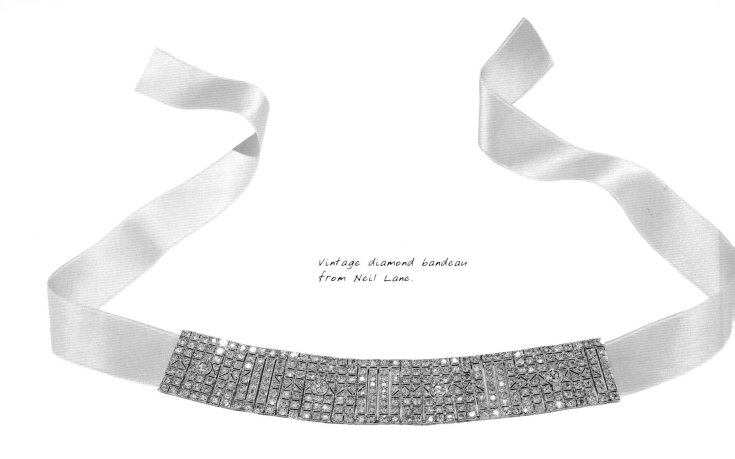

Vintage diamond bandeau
from Neil Lane.

Van Cleef & Arpels
Haricot clip.

happily ever afterword

A wedding doesn't just happen. Countless things must be done to make the celebration the right expression of a couple's love and style. In the whirl of it all—the music, flowers, cake — the jewels should not be overlooked. They may seem like small objects, but actually they are so much bigger and brighter than anything else. There is truth to that golden yarn — diamonds *are* forever.

Couples moving through the labyrinth of details, from the proposal and engagement ring to the wedding day, can refer back to the facts in this book to give them confidence before buying jewelry. Leafing through the legends, lore, and celebrity anecdotes will provide ideas, rest, and relaxation. And above all, every bride and groom should take time to appreciate that they are becoming part of a gloriously beautiful tradition.

many thanks!

A large, tireless troupe helped us get *With This Ring* to the altar. Some were there from the proposal to the Happily Ever Afterword. Others came to our aid in crucial moments. Everyone was generous and good-spirited and we thank you all.

A heartfelt thanks to Ralph Esmerian, whose passion for jewelry is an inspiration always, and everyone else at the R. Esmerian, Inc., executive suite, Trudy Tripolone, Saralee Smithwick, John Ullmann, and Janet Bliss. Across the concourse at *In Style* we would like to thank the brilliant and charming Charla Lawhon and her amazing editors, especially Cindy Weber Cleary, Hal Rubenstein, Jackie Goewey, Clare McHugh, and Honor Brodie, all of whom have taught us so much. A sincere thanks to *People*'s Martha Nelson (those lucky people), who convinced us a book on wedding jewelry was the right thing to do. We owe a deep debt of gratitude to Sally Morrison, the director of the Diamond Information Center and the godmother of this book, as well as her sparkling and efficient team, Kelly McMahon, Amanda Patterson, and Lauren Locascio. A very special thanks must be given to the super-smart and hilarious Linda Buckley of Tiffany & Co., who was a rock, indeed a diamond, every day. To commuter Carol Brodie Gelles of Winston, thanks for disrupting the club car. Many thanks to Fred Leighton and his team for making sure the book sparkled plenty. Big thank-yous go to the indefatigable Neil Lane, always available on the other end of the cell phone, early morning, noon, and late night. We are grateful for the unique assistance of the

Earl Spencer, Sean Ferrer, Madonna, Tim Mendelson, and Elizabeth Taylor. To Nancy Trichter, who has been our superstar agent forever, thanks for the courage under financial and emotional fire. For all our wonderful friends and families — you know who you are — we love you and thank you more than words can express.

The sun never set on the *With This Ring* team. In our illustrator, Sukhee Ko, based in Korea, we found a true Seoul sister. Thanks so much for your beautiful work. Darrin Haddad, who photographed most of the jewelry in the book, was calm, cool, and collected in the face of a sea of engagement rings. A million thanks; we will never forget it. A shout of thanks goes to our delightful Seattle-based designer, Nina Barnett, who juggled illustrations, celebrity photos, text, and jewels and never let a ball fall. At the big bird, Bulfinch, headquarters in New York, we are deeply grateful to our patient editor, Betty Wong, who showed us how to spread our wings further and make the book fly and sing, and to our enthusiastic publisher, Jill Cohen, for making sure the book had all the best plumage for its flight into the world.

Penny and Marion
New York City, 2004

photo credits

index

E

earrings:
  as wedding day jewelry, 27, 85, 86, 89, 149, 156–59
  as wedding presents, 69, 75, 76, 146, 147
Edward VIII (king), 42, 72, 73
Elara, 159
Elizabeth II (queen), 36, 37, 76, 80, 81
Ellen, Caroline, 137
emerald cut, 102, 112, 115
emeralds, symbolism of, 12–13
engagement rings:
  alternatives in, 132–39
  buying of, 128–30, 150
  celebrities and, 33–67
  design elements of, 102–27
  designing your own, 141–43
  history of, 11–17
  personal style and, 98, 100, 102
  ring glossary, 100–101
  trading up, 131
England, 11, 12, 16, 25, 27
engraving, 13–14, 15, 42, 73, 145, 150
Esmerian, R., 105, 113, 134
eternity bands, 34, 44, 47, 102, 132, 136–38, 150
Europe, 12, 21, 113

F

facets, 104
fancy, 126
fancy color diamonds, 104
fancy cut, 104
fancy dark, 126
fancy deep, 126
fancy intense, 126
fancy vivid, 126
Farrow, Mia, 52, 53
feather, 124
Felsen, Suzanne, 109

Ferrer, Mel, 46, 47
fingers, ring fingers, 11, 18–19
fire, the (of diamond), 104
flawless (FL), 104, 124, 135
flaws, 124
4Cs, 104, 122–25, 130, 136
France, 19
Francis I (king), 21

G

Galliano, John, 94
garnets, 20
Garrard, 55, 76, 86
gem grading reports, 104, 122, 124, 128–29
Gemological Institute of America, 128–29
George VI (king), 80
Georgian heart pendant, 94, 95
gimmel engagement rings, 13–14
girdle, 104
Giuliano, Arthur, 23
Giuliano, Carlo, 23
gold:
  engagement rings and, 12, 105
  signet-style rings, 48
  wedding bands and, 150
Goldberg, William, 117, 130
gold wreaths, 25
Greene, Leslie, 138
grooms, 69, 145
Gübelin of Zurich, 47
Gumdrop ring, 108

H

hair ornaments, 94, 95, 149, 161–62
See also tiaras
Hepburn, Audrey, 46, 47

I

inclusions, 104, 124
India, 25, 26, 113
internally flawless (IF), 124
Ireland, 15
iron, 11, 12

J

Jewish wedding rings, 14, 19

K

Karch, Karen, 139
Kashmir sapphires, 135
Katz, Martin, 116, 124, 129
Kay, Scott, 112
Kelly, Grace, 28, 32, 34–35, 74-75, 84–85
Kennedy, Caroline, 88, 89
Kennedy, Jackie, 50, 51, 82, 83, 89
Kennedy, John F., 50, 51
Kennedy, Joseph P., 82
key engagement ring, 12
King, John, 129–30
Knot of Hercules necklace, 20
Kretchmer, Steven, 109
Krupp diamond, 48
Kwiat, 112, 157

L

Lacroix, Christian, 93
Lane, Neil, 63, 66, 94, 115, 157, 162
left hand, 18
Leighton, Fred:
  acorn comb, 161
  cushion-cut diamond, 116
  earrings, 159
  hair ornaments, 94, 95
  marquise-cut diamonds, 64, 114
  tiara, 93
  on white diamonds, 130

About the Authors

Penny Proddow and Marion Fasel are Contributing Editors, Fine Jewelry and Watches, for *In Style*. Their other books include *Bejeweled: Great Designers, Celebrity Style;* and *Hollywood Jewels: Movies, Jewelry, Stars.*

Illustrator

Sukhee Ko has created witty, incisive fashion illustrations for clients such as Tiffany & Co., Gianni Versace, and Air France, as well as *Vogue, GQ, Harper's Bazaar,* and *Marie Claire* in Korea. She is a professor at the Samsung Art and Design Institute, and lives in Seoul, Korea.

Photographer

Darrin Haddad has been a still life photographer in New York City for nine years. Some of his clients include Sony, Tommy Hilfiger, American Express, *In Style,* and *House & Garden.*